RICH MAN POOR BANK

RICH MAN POOR BANK

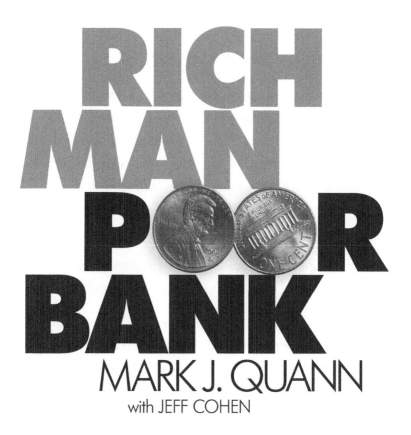

MARK J. QUANN
with JEFF COHEN

Los Angeles

ACKNOWLEDGEMENT

*It has been an unbelievable journey to write this book
over the past four years, and at times I felt like it would
never be finished. I would like to first thank my incredible wife
Rebecca, as being married to a workaholic, financial advisor,
entrepreneur, and author can be challenging at times.
For her never-ending support, I will always be grateful.*

*To my friend and co-author Jeff Cohen who dedicated
his time and energy assisting in the creation of this book.
I would not have finished without his help.*

*To my consultant and friend Mike Metzler for guiding
me through the process of writing my first book, developing
a marketing plan, and for spending all those hours at
Starbucks helping me each step of the way.*

For more information, book orders, corporate discount plans,
media and speaking engagements:

Orders: www.richmanpoorbank.com/book
Facebook: www.facebook.com/richmanpoorbank
Email: mark@richmanpoorbank.com
Blog: www.richmanpoorbank.com

CONTENTS

PART TWO: BANKS NO MORE

For my parents, Ray and Christine Quann,
who always encouraged me and believed that
I can achieve anything I put my mind to.

INTRODUCTION

I was born in 1977. Things were different then. The average cost of a house was around $49,000, and the average personal income was $15,000 a year. A gallon of gasoline was $0.60. The cost of living increased around 6.5% that year (commonly known as inflation) and the banks were paying around 5% interest in savings accounts at your local banks. Yes, when I was born, bank savings actually grew with the rate of inflation, and all that was required to grow your money was to deposit it into a savings account.

Times have changed.

To understand how I came to write a book about banking, it's necessary to tell you a bit about myself and my family. We are from Toronto, Canada, where my father was a mason. The 1994 Northridge earthquake motivated my family to immigrate to California, where we established a business rebuilding the thousands of chimneys that had come crashing down in the disaster.

We left the snow and cold for warm weather, less taxes, capitalism, and a free market economy. We arrived in the

"Land of Sunshine and Opportunity," without a Green Card among us. Like so many immigrants, we came here as visitors with the intention of staying, ready and willing to work hard to achieve the American Dream.

We had to start over again, and for me, mixing concrete in the land of sunshine was a daily occurrence. The sunshine was far hotter than expected, and the work was indeed very hard. My father perfected the art of masonry and my mother took care of us. My dad would joke with me, "Mixing concrete in 100 degrees builds character!"

I soon decided that I had built enough character and abandoned the family business to go back to Canada to seek higher education.

Returning to Canada was my first real introduction to the banking system. I found myself standing in line to complete submissions for student loans. Next, we were corralled to a booth where thousands of us filled in our first credit card applications. "There is no harm in just applying and it will help you build your credit," is what we were told. With each solicitation, we would get a free T-shirt and a two liter bottle of soda. Like thousands of other students, I completed multiple applications. Unfortunately, there was no booth explaining the power of compounding interest.

Despite attending business school, not once did I attend a

class that educated me on how money actually works. In fact, I studied many highly complex statistical formulas, but never once was I provided any real life financial education. Today, I don't give any credit to my college education for my financial success, as it was not until after I left school that I started to truly understand money. In fact, attending college gave me a greater understanding of why the world continues to struggle—and why so few actually win financially.

Finally, when I was to graduate, my career counselor advised me, "You might consider a start-up position at a bank for $30,000 a year, and climb the corporate ladder."

"$30,000 a year? *Are you crazy?*"

I calculated all my debt and realized it would take me decades to pay off my three credit cards and student loans. I felt scammed. I had been suckered into accumulating a huge debt. The thought of working for the bank—to pay back debt to the bank—to support a system of perpetual debt made me sick to my stomach.

I left Canada and returned to California. Soon after getting settled in Los Angeles, I found myself standing in the lobby of one of the big banks. My parents had been customers of a major American bank for years, and in many ways we considered it our family bank. I remember the teller smiling and I smiled back. I couldn't help it, her friendliness was infectious. She was genuinely happy to see that I was following in the family footsteps—to become a "valued customer."

I would discover much later that many employees of the big banks lack financial education like so many others of the working class. Ironic, but true.

Within a few years I met my wife, Rebecca, and we bought our first home, a condominium in Van Nuys, California. And yes, I secured my first mortgage and watched as my credit score began to rise as I made each payment. And with real estate prices skyrocketing, I soon saw an opportunity to sell my home—to get out of debt. With this sale, I managed to completely pay off all my Canadian student loans and old credit cards. It was a great day. I remember what a wonderful feeling it was to send that last payment in the mail.

We were now in a one bedroom apartment in Burbank, with no more financial ties to Canada.

But like so many, within a few years, I found myself even deeper in debt. I was living the illusion of the American Dream—that is to say, I was a great consumer, spending much of my earnings on entertainment and lifestyle, while charging up my credit cards and saving money in the bank. And before long, we had purchased a larger home in Pasadena and were borrowing on an equity line for renovations. And this time around, I owed money to multiple banks and credit card companies within the United States. Every time I went to the mailbox, it was filled with enticing offers for more credit cards, many even at 0%.

Feeling increasingly frustrated, I knew it would be necessary to ask myself different questions if I were ever to find a true path to financial security. And what I would eventually discover is that I had the capacity to think outside the box. The questions I asked would set me on a path to a wholly unexpected career, and ultimately toward financial freedom.

I first asked the question, "Why is it that all the education I have been given about money seems to lead me back into debt?"

This inspired me to ask more and I wrote them down:

"Why does the system require Americans (and Canadians) to get into debt in order to build their credit?"

"What are the banks doing with the money in my savings account?"

"Is it good advice to take children to the bank to open up a checking and savings account?"

"What happens to the money when the bank forecloses on a home?"

"Is it possible to save money and build credit without ever borrowing from or saving in a bank?"

"Where do rich people save their money, if not in a bank?"

"Why should the government need to provide regulations to prevent the banks from enslaving all Americans in debt?"

"Why are the big banks becoming richer each year while American families are becoming poorer?"

To find answers to these questions, I decided to abandon the traditional educational system and began to read books about money, entrepreneurship, business, banking, debt, and investing. I was intent on acquiring a strong financial education—without the help of the banks. The more books I read and the more I learned, the more I began to understand how money actually works.

My readings challenged my beliefs and I soon began to question everything I thought I knew about money. I had found my passion and wanted to learn more. New questions arose, and as time went on, I began to find clarity and direction after years of struggling with debt.

I will attempt to answer the above questions throughout this book, as well as share the journey that led me to my answers.

I sit with hundreds of families a year and talk about money. You're not alone if you feel you don't understand the subject. Money is one of the most misunderstood subjects in the world today. To enhance your understanding, several chapters will introduce you to a family shouldering tremendous responsibilities: three young children to care for, a heavy mortgage on a home, managing credit card and auto loans, and much of their savings held in savings accounts and CDs in the bank. The profile of this young family is very common in America, and is similar to the hundreds of families that I have helped over the years. Their questions will likely reflect many of your own and thus bring a clearer understanding of the concepts that follow.

As you read, understand, and apply the information herein, you will become far more educated than 99% of the population on the subject of money.

PART ONE

THE DEBT MATRIX

*In a time of universal deceit, telling
the truth is a revolutionary act.*

–George Orwell

Chapter 1

THE BIG BANKS: AN OVERVIEW

*The money powers prey upon the nation
in times of peace and conspire against it in times of adversity.
It is more despotic than a monarchy, more insolent than autocracy,
and more selfish than bureaucracy. It denounces as public enemies
all who question its methods or throw light upon its crimes. I have
two great enemies, the Southern Army in front of me and
the bankers in the rear. Of the two, the
one at my rear is my greatest foe.*

–Abraham Lincoln

L et's begin by taking an inside look at modern banking today, and see how it has changed from when I was a born in 1977.

Today, the largest banks in America are paying an average of 0.05% on savings accounts and lending your hard-earned money back to you at interest rates of 10-24%, or higher. They also use your savings and invest for personal profit. To make things worse, they are constantly looking for ways to charge you additional fees. If your savings account falls too low, they'll charge you a fee. If you talk with a teller, they'll charge you a fee. If your account goes into overdraft, they'll charge you a fee. If you use the wrong ATM, they'll charge you a fee.

Being a customer of big banking has become a game of "dodge-a-fee," as they change the rules any time they want.

In addition to bank fees, households that have credit card debt, on average, carry close to $16,000 with average interest rates of 16%. If you're reading this and thinking, "Thank goodness I don't have any credit card debt," that suggests that one of your neighbors may be carrying $32,000 in credit card debt, likely at an interest rate of 12-24%. If your neighbor pays $800 each month for the next five years, they will not quite get out of debt, and they will have paid more than $20,000 in interest.

And where does all that interest go? To the ever-deepening

pockets of the Wall Street bankers, never again to return to our communities. If anything does return, it will likely arrive by mail in the form of thousands of "pre-approved" credit card offers.

What I concluded after looking at all of this is that big banking is no longer championing capitalism at all. I learned that the banking system in the United States (and the rest of the world) is actually corrupting the true spirit of capitalism.

I found out that the banks have built a perpetual debt matrix—where the banks win and the financially uneducated lose.

Fortunately, you can win, but in order to do so you must raise your Financial IQ. Your Financial IQ is how well you understand the language of money. To understand this language you must first understand the words. When you understand the words, you can eventually speak the language. Finally, when you become fluent in the language of money, you can begin taking control of your money rather than having it control you.

Chapter 2

JACK AND ELLEN: THE FIRST MEETING

If you got out of bed this morning and went to work because you wanted to, you are in control of money. If you got out of bed this morning because you had to, money is in control of you. Even in the wealthiest nation in the world, 99% of the population is being controlled by money."

–Steve Siebold

met Jack one Friday afternoon while standing in line at Starbucks. We had been chatting about the increase in the price of a cup of coffee.

Jack commented, "Coffee alone will put you into debt. They should call this place 'Fourbucks.'"

I laughed, took him up on the joke, "Especially your Frappuccino Latte."

While adding cream to my coffee, I learned that Jack was an accountant, and we exchanged business cards.

Later that week, Jack and his wife Ellen were sitting across from me in my office. They both looked to be in their mid to late thirties. An attractive, spirited couple, curious but uncertain. I let them know that I had no other appointments scheduled until three, so we could relax, get to know each other a bit.

I discovered that they lived in a small three bedroom house in Burbank.

They have two sons and one daughter: 12, 10, and 7 years of age.

"Jack meets his clients at his office a mile or so from here," said Ellen.

"And Ellen has an administrative job at St. Joseph's Hospital—three twelve hour shifts a week. We manage our work schedules so we can trade off taking care of the kids without hiring a part-time nanny. We chose not to put any of the kids in day care." Ellen continued. "My mom's got the kids for the day, but I should be getting back soon. So, I'm pretty good with numbers and Jack can tell you everything about taxes. I believe we're pretty much up to speed on our finances, right sweetheart?"

"Pretty much," Jack replied.

There was a pause in the conversation. Ellen broke the silence.

"To be honest, Mark, it wasn't my idea to come here, but Jack had a good feeling about you the other day, so I relented." Ellen laughed, a bit nervously.

"Well, since we're all here, if there's anything I can do to help, I will," I said.

Jack answered quickly. "We have a bit of debt, and coffee aside, we would love to dig ourselves out of it."

Ellen looked at her husband. "We always make our payments on time."

"That we do. Our mortgage, one car payment, and paying what we can to bring down the credit cards."

"I'm really not comfortable talking about this, Jack," Ellen said.

"This is a difficult time for so many families." I said, "I can tell you that you're not alone. Talking about money is a sensitive subject, would you agree?"

Jack and Ellen fell silent for a moment.

"Clearly," Ellen said, and I could feel her opening up a bit.

"I believe I can help you, but for that to be possible, I would need to gather the details of your financial picture the next time we get together."

Jack turned to his wife. "Would that be alright, Ellen?"

"Well, I suppose, if nothing we say leaves this office."

I smiled, "If I do my job right, Ellen, you'll have nothing to lose and everything to gain."

Ellen smiled openly for the first time. "Alright. Might as well give it a shot."

I began asking questions about their short, mid, and long term financial goals.

Ellen interrupted. "Mark, I suppose I should have asked when we started. What do you charge for your services?"

"My services are entirely complimentary, Ellen. And unlike most financial professionals, I take the time to educate my clients about money first. If they understand money thoroughly, they can make better informed financial decisions after they leave my office."

"How do you make money then?" Jack asked. "Are you a non-profit?"

"No," I responded and began to chuckle. "I actually do

quite well by moving people's money to places where it works hard for them, while reducing their taxes and debt. Most people have money work against them for their entire lives."

"Okay, then how do we make our money work hard for us?" Ellen was beginning to enjoy herself.

"I can teach you how to make your money work for you, but I must warn you, my advice will likely be very different from what you have been previously told to do. In fact, what if my advice is the opposite of what you have learned in the past, would you still be open to hearing what I have to say?"

"Well that depends," Jack responded. "What do you mean?"

Ellen jumped in, "Jack, first things first. We just want to get out of debt and as I told you, Mark, we're doing everything right. We both have post-graduate degrees and stable careers. We have money in savings accounts and we have an "800" credit score. Our mortgage is thirty year fixed and we send in extra principal payments every month. Our car loan is around 6% interest, and although we do have some credit card debt, we never just pay the minimums. Jack adds money to his IRA and I have a 401(k) at my job to save on taxes, and we have CDs at our bank for the kids' college funds. Jack has a thirty year term insurance policy that is quite reasonable. We're actually pretty good savers compared to most. And unlike the stock market, the money at the bank is insured."

"So why are we not getting ahead?" Jack asked.

"It's only a matter of time, dear."

It was time for me to ask some questions—some of the same ones I had asked myself years ago. "Can I be completely candid with you?"

Ellen paused a moment, "Why not?"

"Almost everything you are currently doing, I do the opposite with my personal finances. And I teach my clients to do the same. Does that surprise you?"

Jack responded, "Are you suggesting that everything we're doing is wrong?" He managed an attempt at a joke. "How is that possible, I'm an accountant?"

"'Wrong' is a strong word, and I wouldn't go that far. I would tell you that, like most Americans, you have been steered in the wrong direction. I would imagine that you know more about taxes than I do and perhaps you share a few tricks to save your clients some money each year. My focus is entirely different."

Ellen was becoming increasingly curious. "How do you mean?"

"At the risk of being dramatic, I believe that almost everything you have been taught in school and from well-meaning family members and friends—virtually all the education you have been provided about money has been manipulated and corrupted. The result of this is that your money has been put to work for someone else rather than you. I can show you how to get your money working for you, but it may require abandoning much of the information you have been taught about money. If you are open to change, I can help you."

"We're open to listening" Jack responded. Ellen nodded in agreement.

"One of my first memories about money," I smiled, "I believe I was barely a teen when my mom and dad brought me down to the bank to open my very first checking and savings account with a crisp ten dollar bill. I remember holding my first book of checks and a debit card. I felt like a grown up. We laugh about it now, but this was the biggest mistake my parents ever made in teaching me about money."

Jack was amused, but surprised. "My father did the same thing. We opened up a savings account and my credit has been aces ever since."

"I remember one of my friend's parents taking her to the bank," said Ellen, "so I wanted my mom to do the same for me. We all went through that."

"Exactly," I said, "and all your children will grow up to do the same thing for their children, and so on. What I can tell you is that savings accounts are guaranteed to lose money, one hundred percent of the time. And unless we make a radical change, the vast majority of Americans will remain on this entirely misguided financial path—for generations.

"What change are you suggesting?" Ellen asked.

"The sole purpose of the banks is to make your money work for them, not you. I save quite a lot of money but none of it is in a bank. And I wouldn't take advice from any banker about what to do with my money either."

"Now I'm confused," said Ellen.

"As was I—at the beginning. My sole intention, Ellen, is to bring you clarity, a new direction, and ultimately, peace of mind in all areas regarding your family's financial life. I can show you that new path the next time we meet."

"I look forward to hearing more," said Ellen.

"As do I," said Jack.

We scheduled our next meeting the following Tuesday morning, shook hands, and parted.

Chapter 3

FINANCIAL EDUCATION

The number one problem in today's generation and economy is the lack of financial literacy."

–Alan Greenspan

n the early years, much of my education was obtained in the school of hard knocks. Most everyone in America has attended the same school, and for many, the hard knocks have come in the form of bankruptcy, foreclosure, and all to often in divorce.

Today, what worries me most is that even those considered highly-educated have been taught almost nothing useful about money. Every day, I sit with doctors, attorneys, small business owners, teachers, accountants, financial professionals, and even professors of business and economics—and teach them about money. In fact, I estimate that today only about 1% of the population actually understands the subject well.

Perhaps you are asking, "How is it possible that 99% of the population doesn't understand money?" You may recall the very first question I asked myself in my early years: "Why is the only 'financial education' provided in school about how to borrow money?" Now I can answer that question, and the answer is alarming to most who hear it. The banks' very existence is based on seducing the American people to borrow more and more money, thereby keeping them in debt throughout their lives. To maintain this course, it is necessary to keep the public unaware of the dire consequences of debt, and the banks must keep the population ignorant of how money actually works. If Americans were educated about how money works, the bankers would become poorer as more Americans become financially free.

Back in Canada, the girls took "Home Economics 101," and the boys, "Manual Arts" in 7th and 8th grades. The girls could bake a cake and sew a button; the boys knew how to make a napkin holder, but neither had a clue on how to manage money.

Even today I have visited a "Finance Park," which claim to educate children about how money works, only to find out that much of the funding for the parks comes from the biggest banks. I did not find real financial education there—at least not the financial education that the rich teach to their children. I only saw "banking education," with the biggest banks indoctrinating hundreds of thousands of kids with mis-education about money. One employee of the park, when asked about the substance of the training, said, "Yup, unfortunately our bread is buttered by the banks."

The question you might be asking today is, "Why are the true fundamentals of managing money not taught to our children?"

I am of the firm belief that the banking lobby is so powerful, it assures that basic financial education is not available in our elementary, middle, and high schools. Ironically, I can and do teach how money works in a matter of two short one hour meetings.

The reason it is a bad idea to take children to the bank, is that bankers know very well that children will develop an emotional attachment to the first bank where their parents help them open a checking and savings account. And an offer for a credit card harbors the belief:

"My bank believes in my future."

And so a lifetime of brainwashing begins.

"You need to get good credit," and "Saving in the bank is the key to your future," are the seeds for a lifetime of debt to the banks.

I would be very curious to know the answers to the following questions:

Are you still a customer with the same bank where your parents opened your first checking and savings account? Did your bank make you feel grown up when you applied for your first credit card? Did they call you "credit-worthy?"

"Credit worthy" is a term the bank uses to make you feel "worthy" of something. In this case, worthy to start the process of burying yourself in debt, preferably for the rest of your life.

In college I had virtually no income, yet somehow succumbed to the bank's pitch of making me feel worthy of incurring a very large credit card debt as well as substantial student loans, with no idea at all of how I was to pay them back.

Our schools don't teach the basics of investing and they certainly don't teach the benefits of living with little or no debt. They should be the first line of defense against the lies of the bankers. As long as the banks control the credit system and parents and teachers teach children how to get good credit by going into debt, it is no wonder why our economy is in its current financial crisis.

I am always impressed and inspired by people who dedicate their lives to helping others, and especially those who guide children. It has been my privilege to have met a man named Eliel Swinton, who runs the Carpe Diem Sports Academy (www.cpdsportsacademy.com). Carpe Diem translated simply means, "Seize the Day."

Eliel, a former professional football player and now CEO and founder of the academy, counsels young athletes from ages six and up. In addition to mentoring these kids in sport, Eliel guides them in all areas of their lives: instilling leadership, how to be a part of a community, and what it means to be successful both on-and-off the field.

My role at the academy is to educate these kids about money.

This is no easy task, and even my best efforts can only make a limited impact in a country built on debt, when even their parents celebrate spending what they do not have.

Thirty-seven states teach mandatory sex education. Only four states offer financial education as an elective. So our children are destined to grow up financially illiterate, not knowing the difference between a stock and a bond, what a mutual fund is, how rates of return work, and most critically, how and where to save money.

All children have a right to financial education, beginning at a young age, and much of that education needs to come from their parents. But how can it come from parents who don't understand finances themselves?

I've found that kids are fascinated by the adult world, and as long as my lessons are to the point, clear, fun, and simple to understand even by six year olds, then my message will be absorbed. Regardless of children's short attention span, they are still much easier to teach than adults, who are often brainwashed by the banks' incessant media campaigns—which are very hard to combat.

If children are given good financial education, they will be positioned to make sound financial decisions later in life. Rather than living their lives in constant financial turmoil, I am certain that many of our kids, with sound financial education, will have a good chance of achieving financial freedom. The banking lobby will fight financial education tooth and nail because their survival depends on the next generation's ignorance. In fact, I believe that the banking industry sees financial education as their greatest threat— a weapon of mass destruction that could shatter their "debt matrix."

Fighting the mega banks' control over people is the central message of this book, and a fight I believe is worth waging to the core of my soul.

Unfortunately, during my journey, I have learned that the financial education provided to Americans (and the rest of the world), has been corrupted, manipulated, distorted, twisted, and turned inside out—so that only a very few are allowed to win—while the poor and middle classes are destined to lose. The financial advice provided to most Americans benefits only the banker, while depriving everyone else.

To make things worse, this corrupted financial information has been adopted by the masses as truth. It has been passed down from generation to generation—keeping the vast majority of Americans struggling financially.

Today, I have found that most Americans fall into only two categories: those who think they understand money, but are simply running fast in the wrong direction; and those who sense the information they have been provided has been corrupted and are seeking real financial education.

The corrupted financial information widely available to the

masses benefits two groups: the banks and the government. And as you read further, you may even conclude that the interests of the banks and the government have become one and the same.

Chapter 4

JACK AND ELLEN: CLARITY

*An investment in knowledge
pays the best interest."*

–Benjamin Franklin

W hen Jack and Ellen arrived Tuesday morning, they brought coffee and three Starbuck's "Bistro Boxes," as well as a handful of files. Jack placed the documents on my desk. "It's all here, Mark. Bank, credit card, CD and car loan statements, mortgage info. Everything."

Ellen sat herself down and said, "Okay Mr. Quann, we're all in. Can you stop the bleeding?" Jack and I laughed.

"I believe I can, Ellen," I said, "and given the challenges people face today, it's important to maintain a sense of humor. But before I gather the details, I want to continue the process of dispelling confusion, to bring clarity to how money works. Would that be alright with you?"

"If nothing else," Jack said, "I'm discovering that there are more than a few gaps in my knowledge."

"And I've made the decision to be open from here on in, Mark," Ellen said.

I pulled out a sheet of paper and drew a box.

"If we were to take Americans from all walks of life and put them inside a box, what percent do you think understand how to manage their money effectively?"

"Five percent?" asked Ellen.

"More like one percent. Out of 1,000 people, only about 10 get the best financial education, leaving the 990 with no access to the best advice.

"What is the best advice?" asked Ellen.

"Well, Ellen, the wealthy know how to do three things with their money: They get higher rates of returns on all their money; they know how to never lose money, and they know how to invest in tax-exempt investments. About one percent of the population gets the best financial advice.

"That wouldn't be us," said Jack.

"Not yet," I smiled.

"Alright then, what about the rest of the 990 people? Who helps them? You?" asked Ellen.

"Not just me, but a growing number like me.

"Unfortunately, much of the financial industry as it currently exists only helps the very wealthy, while the rest of the population is left out in the cold. And yes, that's what I do. I've chosen to help the 990 that do not have access to the best financial information. And the best financial information is not available from your bank, of that I am certain."

"Are you recommending that people take their money out of the banks entirely?"

"Absolutely, and as we go forward, it will become increasingly apparent why."

"And in the right places," Ellen commented. "This would be investing in the market? That's when I get nervous. We don't want to lose what little we have in savings."

"I understand," I replied. "But my job is to manage your risk and even provide opportunities to invest where you cannot lose your principal whatsoever."

"How is that possible?" asked Jack.

"I promise that we'll explore this as we go forward."

"Tax exempt environments?" asked Ellen. "How is that possible?"

I smiled, "The affluent understand these three criteria very well, and you and Jack deserve to know them too. But let's begin with a little formula that has to do with rates of return. Allow me to tell you a little story:

A reporter once asked Albert Einstein what was his most important discovery."

"Compound interest!" Einstein answered mischievously.

"What! Not the law of relativity? Not E=Mc²?"

"Do you understand these things? Do you employ them in your day-to-day life?" Einstein asked.

"I suppose not," the reporter replied.

"Exactly, my good man. But if people understood my 'Rule of 72,' it would be the eighth wonder of the world!"

"The 'Rule of 72?' I've never heard of it," Jack said.

"Most people haven't. And all it requires is second grade math. What you do is divide 72 by any rate of return, and the result will tell you how many years it will take for your money to double. This same formula can be used to show the banks how long it will take to double their money when investing your savings for personal profit.

For example, divide 72 by a 1% rate of return. How many times does 1 go into 72?"

"Given my post-graduate class in statistics, I can tell you that the answer is 72," said Jack.

"That's right, Jack! It takes 72 years for your money to double when saved in a bank paying 1%."

"72 years for our money to double!" said Ellen.

I asked them if they knew what rate of return they were earning at their bank, and neither were certain. Jack guessed 1%.

"I can tell you that the average rates of return in savings

accounts at any of the big banks, last I looked, was not 1%, but .05%."

Jack pulled out his iPhone and worked out the result. "I don't think we'll be around to see our money double in 1440 years."

I could see that Jack and Ellen were beginning to connect the dots, so I went on, "and I can tell you that the one percent of Americans who know how to manage and grow their money are not saving it in the banks. Their money is in places where they have rates of return between 6% and 10%, so they are doubling their money in 12, and even 7 years. And that's exactly where I have my money as well."

"Incredible," said Ellen.

"Blame it on Einstein," Jack countered.

"And it doesn't matter if you earn 0.05%, or 4%, you are actually always losing money."

"More bad news?" Ellen said.

"I promise you, Ellen, that as we proceed, you'll come through all of this all the wiser, and in the end, very happy."

"We know you're here to help us, Mark," Jack said.

"To illustrate my point then, let's say for example the bank is being generous, and gives you 1% return on your money. But what if inflation is 4%? Is that 1% still a positive rate of return? Let's do the math. A 1% rate of return minus 4% inflation equals a loss of 3%. Your purchasing power, over the years, continues to decrease dramatically. And remember, whatever little money you earn in interest at the bank is taxed at the highest rates. Yet the banks continue to recommend that you save much of your money in these accounts that guarantee that you'll never get ahead financially. And to make things worse, the government hides the real inflation rate from the American people.

"Makes me want to pack up and join the Wall Street protesters," said Ellen.

"You mentioned that you had a number of CDs," I said. "I happen to know that CDs at all the big banks are paying between 0.1% and 0.5% depending on the term. Divide 72 by 0.5% and your result is approximately 144 years for your money to double. And here is the last thing I will tell you. The banks are not rolling up your hard-earned dollars in a rubber band and keeping it on a shelf until you come in and make a withdrawal. They're investing your money at considerably high rates of return, earning massive profits while you lose, as well as lending it back to you at exponentially high interest rates. I'll leave you with some material on 'fractional reserve banking' as to how this is done. "

"Sounds like a damn Ponzi scheme!" said Jack.

"My conclusion exactly."

"This is terrifying. Because it is so pervasive in our culture, we don't even see we are being scammed," Ellen said.

"I believe we are, Ellen. The fact is, all savings at the banks are scams. Scams to keep your money working hard—working hard for the banks, that is. There are endless scams your banker employs, convincing you to save with them: account minimums, automatic saving programs, CDs as effective retirement plans—all devised to draw you in. I can assure you that none of these are for your benefit. They only benefit the banks."

"You told us that you would give us some financial education. You've certainly kept your promise," said Jack, looking at his wife, who appeared a bit shell-shocked.

"Let me ask you something. Let's go back to our little diagram for a moment. What would it be like to take your bank out of the equation entirely? Keep a little for day-to-day expenses, perhaps a few thousand dollars in your local not-for-profit credit union, and put all the rest of your savings in places with good rates of return. And when investing for the long term, you can have guarantees where you won't lose a penny and as much as possible, in tax-exempt environments."

Ellen's eyes lit up a bit. "That would be great."

"We'll see what we can do then," I said. "Let's have a look at what you've brought in. I'll gather the data and next time we meet, I'll suggest some of those possibilities."

Before they left, I handed them a copy of the pre-published chapters you're now about to read.

"You may find this intriguing," I said. "Won't take you long to read and I would very much value your thoughts on it."

Ellen said, "Thank you, Mark. We'll both have it read before we see you next."

Chapter 5

THE "RULE OF 72" AND THE BIG BANKS

Compound interest is the eighth wonder of the world.
He who understands it, earns it... he who doesn't... pays it.

–Albert Einstein

The "Rule of 72" is not taught in our schools, and to my knowledge, it is not offered in any traditional educational curriculum in the world. Your parents have likely never heard of the rule, yet throughout their lives they've been ruled by it.

And the banks are intent on you remaining ignorant of it, because your knowing the "Rule of 72" will make clear to you how your money sits idle and lazy in your savings accounts and CDs.

Let's apply the "Rule of 72" to discover how many years it will take the major banks in the United States to double your money in some of their "basic" savings accounts.

A typical "Day-To-Day" savings account

Using Einstein's simple formula, dividing 72 by 0.01%, a bank will double your savings approximately every 7,200 years!

A "Savings Plus" savings account

You may have heard of these. At 0.05%, a major bank promises to double your money every 1440 years. Note the words, "Savings Plus." Such branding is frighteningly clever. And "fees may reduce earnings" is often in the small print.

"High Yield" savings accounts

At 0.03%, some of the biggest banks will double your money every 2,400 years. And, with a "Bonus APY" (annual percentage yield) they will bump it up to 0.08% so you can double your money every 900 years. If you deposit $1,000 at birth into this account, eat only fruits and vegetables, and lived longer than anyone in history, you may see your account bursting with $2,000.

"Regular" savings accounts

At 0.01%, the larger banks will double your money every 7,200 years. And in the small print there is always a minimum balance requirement (or a monthly service fee will apply). Look for the fees if you don't maintain the minimum or make too many withdrawals in a month.

At smaller banks, you can earn slightly higher returns, but none keep ahead of inflation, many have hidden fees, and all gains are subject to the highest tax rates.

The results speak for themselves. But this is only the beginning of the story.

Chapter 6

THE TRUTH ABOUT AUTOMATIC SAVINGS PLANS

*How many millionaires do you know who have become wealthy
by investing in savings accounts? I rest my case.*

–Robert G. Allen

Automatic savings plans are becoming increasingly prevalent with all the major banks. They dress up these savings plans with massive advertising budgets, big banners, pretty colors, smiling customers, and persuasive catch phrases.

For example, some of the biggest banks offer a program whereby if you purchase an item with your debit card, they'll transfer a small amount of "change" into your savings account. This is just a ploy to keep more of your money idle within the bank's vault. Every dollar sitting in your savings account gives your banker the opportunity to lend your money to other customers. They will pay you virtually nothing for this, while shelling out your funds to other customers at the highest possible interest rates.

Typical wording to describe this type of account might be something like, "Don't give it a second thought." This suggests you are better off without thinking. So, let's examine some other typical small print to find out what the banks want you to not think about:

"Pays a variable annual percentage yield that is .01%."

You'll be waiting 7,200 years for your money to double.

"Fees may reduce earnings."

Evidently, after they pay you 0.01%, there may be undisclosed fees.

"Patent pending."

Are scams to lock up your money at virtually no rate of return worthy of a patent?

All of the major banks have devised schemes like these to lock up more of your money.

Recently, I've seen another mega bank promoting a very clever, yet devious way to save. Those who have one of these plans are unlikely to read the small print disclosures.

The bank proceeds with the full knowledge that most of their customers lack financial education and will trust them to go forward with any schemes they devise.

This new way to save is promoted with an image of a morning cappuccino and pastry. If you're hungry and like coffee, it all looks quite appealing. You may be asking how these banking executives sleep at night, knowing they make their money by selling the lie that you can make money by "saving" it in a bank.

The answer is: *they buy really expensive silk sheets.*

Your bank's only goal is to lock up your money and pay you nothing—then charge you fees—only to lend it back to you in credit cards, auto loans, and mortgages at the highest possible interest rates.

Every dollar saved at a big bank is simply another dollar to be retained by Wall Street.

It is ironic that many new immigrants arriving to this country keep their money in tin cans in their back yards or under their mattresses, yet we call them ill-informed for not having savings accounts. The irony is that they don't pay $35 overdraft fees and $5 monthly service charges. They buy what they need with cash and their mattresses and tin cans don't offer them credit cards to buy things they can't afford.

The truth is your banker needs your money more than you need your banker. And without your savings and debt, your banker would be in big trouble.

Chapter 7

THE
TRUTH ABOUT
CDs

*The main reason people struggle financially is because
they have spent years in school but learned nothing about money.
The result is that people learn to work for money…
but never learn to have money work for them."*

–Robert Kiyosaki

Your banker understands human nature very well, especially as it relates to money and savings. To procrastinate regarding financial decisions is very common, so your banker says, "Put your money in a CD for a few years and you won't have to worry about it." Sounds reasonable, doesn't it?

A CD is a "certificate of deposit." It is simply a way for your bank to lock up your money for a period of time, typically one to five years. The banker will then pay you a higher rate of return. Just to clarify, you're not getting a high rate of return, simply a higher percentage than you would receive from a regular savings account.

More often than not, the big banks will require substantial minimums before they will open up investment accounts. In many cases, if you don't have a minimum of $250,000, your banker will encourage you to "invest" in a CD. Please note—your money in a CD is not "invested."

They can call it high yield CDs, super savings, whatever. It is not intended to help you grow your money. One example: A 26-month "Special CD Rate" that a major bank is currently offering at 0.20%. Applying the Rule of 72, you'll have to wait 360 years for your money to double. Since none of these accounts keep ahead of inflation and all gains are highly taxed, the banks might be accused of false and misleading advertising. There are no "high yields" and there is nothing whatsoever "special" about these accounts.

"You can save your money in a CD until it grows to meet our investment minimums," is the standard pitch from your smiling banker. Locking away your savings in CDs for one to five years will only make your money available to the bank to invest on its behalf—not yours.

And here's the rub. Your placing $5,000 into a CD, immediately gives your banker the ability to lend $50,000 to other customers, or even back to you, utilizing "fractional" lending practices. (In the next chapter, I will show how banks leverage Middle America's savings into massive profits for themselves.)

Ironically, almost all bank customers have the opportunity to put their money in the same place the bankers put their money—in secure investments that pay far higher interest rates than the banks!

But people trust their bankers and so believe that CDs are effective savings plans. Bankers love them, because once a CD account is opened, that money will sit idle on average for fifteen years, while the bankers use it to make profits for themselves.

That is not the end of the CD story. For even after your hard-earned money is sitting idle in a long-forgotten "auto-renewal" CD account, the bank will look to reduce your interest rate at every opportunity.

Chapter 8

FRACTIONAL RESERVE BANKING

Give a man a gun and he can rob a bank.
Give a man a bank and he can rob the world."

–Unknown

W e can now elaborate on how the banks utilize your savings to amass exponential profits.

"Fractional Reserve Banking" is the practice in which a bank's reserves (the money deposited in the bank) is only a small fraction of their loans and investments. In other words, your bank may lend $10 for every $1 you have deposited in your savings, checking accounts, or CDs.

For a short time in history, "Full Reserve Banking" was practiced, when banks were restricted from lending your savings to other customers. Today, however, banking systems throughout the world use the fractional reserve system.

With fractional reserve banking, the banks essentially create money out of thin air. No actual money is printed and the debt to all Americans is simply logged as a bank entry.

It is very important to know the following: By its nature, the practice of fractional reserve banking expands the money supply.

Here's how: Walk into any major bank and place $100 into a savings account. As soon as your money is in your account, you have given your bank the ability to lend $1,000 to other customers (perhaps an unsuspecting student at 24% interest).

What is important to understand is who needs who. Without your $100, your bank would not legally be able to lend $1,000.

This practice of lending money that does not exist is the true genius of the banking system. A clear example of how this is done:

A good friend at work tells you how she found a "limited-time offer at 0% financing" at a local car dealership. "You've got to take advantage of this deal by this weekend," she tells you. "Zero percent interest to buy a brand new car!"

You think, "How could I possibly go wrong, borrowing money at zero percent?" So you go down to the dealership, secure a loan for $20,000 and buy a new car.

But did the bank actually lend you $20,000? No, they did not. Let's follow the money trail and see what really happened:

Let's assume you have $2,000 in your savings account. Because you saved the $2,000, your bank can now lend your $2,000 back to you, plus another $18,000 of phantom cash. That's $20,000.

When you buy your car, you sign a contract agreeing that you now owe $20,000, but you didn't borrow the money from the auto dealership, you borrowed it from the bank. And the bank only makes an accounting entry for this amount.

The auto dealership's bank accounting entry shows that they now have $20,000 in their account, even though this sum only exists as and entry in a computer. The dealer never took possession of your money at all.

Because the auto dealership now has this phantom $20,000 in their bank account, their bank can lend out an additional $200,000 of non-existent cash to their customers, simply by logging additional bank entries.

And it all began with the bank helping you save $2,000—while offering you zero percent interest on a loan.

Now you understand how this practice inflates the overall money supply without actually printing it and why your bank pays virtually nothing in interest in savings accounts—yet requires 10-20% down when you buy big-ticket items like the American Dream: your home.

Let's follow the money trail once again:

You save $20,000 for a down payment on a $200,000 home. After the $20,000 is deposited, the bank can lend you $180,000, simply by logging a bank entry that you owe that amount plus interest. (And that interest begins to accrue immediately, compounding each day.)

People are of the general impression that when a bank lends money, in this case $180,000, that money actually exists in the bank's reserves. This is simply not the case. The bank has you tied into a 30 year loan on money that does not exist. You are front-loaded with interest payments with little money ever reducing the principal for the first 10 to 20 years. And if you ever default on your loan, the bank will destroy your credit and simply delete the entry that you owe them any money.

Then, they will foreclose on your home.

The mega banks make billions in profit by charging high interest rates, enslaving American families with trillions of dollars that do not exist.

How is this legal?

It is not only legal, it will stay legal until the population learns how fractional reserve banking works. But currently, our schools do not teach it, our teachers do not understand it, our parents do not know of it, and the banks will do whatever they can to keep the vast majority of Americans ignorant of it.

And here's a very real concern that I believe all Americans should understand: If there occurred another economic crisis and too many Americans attempted to remove their money ar the same time, there wouldn't be enough real money at the branches to manage withrawals. This is known as a "run on the banks."

Now that you understand the basic premise of fractional reserve banking, it is important to know how millions of sales representatives around the country bring you even further into debt when you shop for a car, a big-screen TV, or a new wardrobe.

Who are these sales reps at auto dealerships, home

improvement stores, electronics stores or, for that matter, at every major department store with their incredible offers of 0% down with no interest for the first 12 to 18 months, and offering you a discount to apply for credit?

Henchmen of the banks, that's who.

There are literally hundreds of thousands of men and women selling you all kinds of things with these tantalizing offers. Ironically, they are unknowingly and indirectly employed by the banks and credit card companies, and many are neck-deep in debt, taking advantage of these offerings for credit themselves.

Among the most common of the bankers' henchmen are new and used car salesmen. They will stop at nothing to get you into an auto loan at the highest possible price and interest rate.

"Granted, the interest rate will be high the first six months, but we can refinance you when your credit is better," is their manipulative pitch.

Six months later, when your credit is better and you go back to reduce your interest rate, this is the henchman's scripted response: "Unfortunately, the car is currently worth less than what you owe. As much as I wish I could, I simply can't refinance your loan." Regardless of you reminding him what you were told when you made the purchase, you are chained to the high interest rate you agreed to at the point of sale. Many times, this could be 16% or higher.

Three years later, your car is barely worth anything, as it is a rapidly depreciating asset.

Why would these salesmen persuade their fellow hard-working Americans to get further in debt? The answer is simple. If they don't sell you that new car or big-screen TV, they won't make enough money to stay current on their own debt payments. They are just as concerned about ruining their credit as anyone else, so the banks keep this vicious cycle of unending borrowing, bringing in profits from both the salesmen themselves, and all those who buy on credit.

Chapter 9

TOO BIG TO FAIL, AGAIN?

*Since the amount of deposits always exceeds the amount of reserves,
it is obvious that fractional reserve banks cannot possibly pay all of their
depositors on demand as they promise. If depositors en masse attempted
to withdraw more funds than are available in reserves,
the entire house of cards would come crashing down.
This is the very real threat facing some European banks today.*

—Ron Paul

Now that you understand that the banks don't actually have enough real money in their accounts, it brings to mind a question: How would the bank pay me my money if too many customers, in a future economic crisis, were to storm the branches to withdraw their funds all at once?

The banks would then be exposed for the frauds they are—faceless corporations that can charge you fees to borrow your money, while not even keeping it in their accounts.

During times of crisis, many banks have run out of cash when too many customers arrived simultaneously to withdraw their money. This is a "run on the banks," and one such event was a key cause of the Great Depression. At a time when their savings were needed most to keep them from financial ruin, Americans showed up at their branches to get their money, but the banks were not able to pay. The house of cards, built by the bankers of the world, began tumbling down. If you think this could not happen today, have a talk with your banker about the "Notice of Withdrawal" they may demand of you before you can remove your money from your bank.

Banks have now added new clauses to their "Deposit Agreements & Disclosures," when opening savings and checking accounts. In a review of a major bank's disclosures, we found the following clause:

"Federal regulations require us to retain the right to require all savings and interest–bearing checking account depositors to give seven days written notice before making a withdrawal. It is unlikely, however, that we would require this notice."

Your bank has a similar disclosure item.

I believe that if a financial meltdown occurred, too many people in need of their cash will generate a run on the banks. And when they do, they would be denied access to their money.

Once again, a major bank, in their fine print, (a thirty-six thousand word disclosure in this case) has the legal ability to prevent you from withdrawing your money from your accounts. When you need your money the most, your bank may require "seven days written notice."

When asking to see such disclosures, they will tell you, "It is unlikely we will use it."

My question to your banker: "If it is not going to be used, why not remove it from the agreement?"

If I were a customer of big banking, I would make my own run on the bank to withdraw my money immediately.

Now, I'm not suggesting that all of us do this at once, causing an actual financial crisis, but I am looking to orchestrate a well organized, gradual removal of all of your money from the mega banks, and the closure of their doors forever. Shifting your money to credit unions is one very powerful thing that we can do.

I understand that this may be seen as a radical position, but I am quite convinced that the banking industry is chipping away at the very fabric of true capitalism and what can be a flourishing middle class. It is time for us to take action.

Chapter 10

PLASTIC BANKING

*When you get in debt
you become a slave.*

–Andrew Jackson

America's most common debt to the banks is through the money pit accrued on credit cards. They are an insidious habit. Those households with credit card debt carry an average of $16,000, at an average interest rate of 16%. These interest payments export billions of dollars from your community and benefit only a small few on Wall Street.

In the credit card industry, one of the most brilliant schemes designed to keep Middle America in debt involves simple mathematical equations to bring about the greatest amount of profits for the banks. These equations result in accomplishing four very important goals for the big banks:

1. Get the greatest number of credit cards into the hands of consumers.

2. Set the highest possible balances on those cards (even if at an initial offering of zero percentage rate–it doesn't matter).

3. Increase the interest rates as high as possible and add fees and penalties to increase profits.

4. Maintain the cardholder's debt until death or bankruptcy.

The idea is to set some cheese in a trap and when the mice take the bait, then snap! These mice, however, are oftentimes college students and average American families who only thought they were getting a piece of cheese.

One such strategy used in the past is to reduce the

minimum payment—to extend the time it takes consumers to get out of debt.

Let's use the example of households that carry an average of $10,000 of credit card debt, with a minimum payment of 5%, or $500. They would not likely charge more on the card, because they could not afford the increased payments. The idea was to reduce the minimum payment to 2%, or $200 on the same $10,000 balances. The banks knew that many consumers would then be inclined to charge 2½ times more on their card, or $25,000, and still have the same $500 minimum payment. These massive new balances meant that it would take decades to pay off the cards—if ever, and so result in huge profits for the banks.

And today, the big banks are currently working diligently to place as many cards into the hands of American consumers as possible.

There is an emerging belief that having only one credit card is not enough. In fact, Americans hold over six hundred million credit cards, and many people carry seven in their wallet at a time. Advertising sound bites such as, "Never leave home without it!" instill the belief that credit cards are necessary to survive.

Every time you swipe your credit card, not only is your bank charging the merchandiser a hefty surcharge, but it also has you unknowingly abetting in yet another scheme of creating more phantom money with a simple entry in their database—registered as your debt plus applicable interest.

The banks have been known to increase this interest any time they want, and until recently, there has been nothing Americans could do about it.

Millions of Americans have experienced the shock when opening the envelope of a credit card statement with an exponentially higher interest rate caused by one day's late payment—even on another card. This practice is called "universal default." Here is how it works:

First, your credit card company sends you a notice stating, "We are decreasing your available credit." Soon after, you receive a second notice, "Because you have used too much of your available credit (because they just reduced your credit limit), please note an increased interest rate." Don't be surprised if they raise your rate from 16% to 29.99%.

When you go to your bank for an explanation, they will tell you that their hands are tied because you've become a "higher credit risk." They'll refer you to the original agreement that you signed, which has convoluted language only a lawyer (who wrote it) could understand.

They'll tell you that because of a "decrease in your credit worthiness," the door is left open to increase your interest rate for almost any reason at all. If you didn't feel bad enough coming to your branch, you'll feel worse on departing.

There was a time when many of the current schemes of the credit card companies were actually not permitted in the United States. In fact, 24% interest was illegal and interest rates could go no higher than 12%.

Things changed with the rampant inflation in the late 1970s. The Federal Reserve, (the "Granddaddy" of inflation) increased interest rates to double digits to try to slow the economy.

At the time, rates being charged to banks were up to 18%. How could a bank borrow money at 18%, lend it out at 12%, and still make a profit? They couldn't.

But South Dakota was in economic trouble, and needed to attract banks and jobs to their state. They decided to remove the cap on interest rates a bank could charge their customers on credit cards. This brought banks lining up to set up offices in South Dakota. Shortly thereafter, a court decision allowed the credit card companies to export their uncapped interest rates to other states. South Dakota's fortunes improved, because now their new laws opened the doors for credit card companies to send unregulated applications all over the country.

A major national bank came to the state to embrace this new, very profitable loophole in the deregulation of the industry. Before long, all the mega banks began sending out applications by the tens of millions all over the country.

Over the years since the 1970s, inflation pulled back to reasonable levels, and the Federal Reserve reduced interest rates charged to banks. Despite this, even with reduced rates to borrow money, the banks had developed a taste for charging 24% interest on credit card debt, and few adjustments were made to benefit their customers.

Applying Einstein's simple formula, 72 divided by 24 equals 3. That means that the bank is doubling credit card balances every 3 years, while doubling the money in your savings account every 1440 years!

When presenting this fact to thousands of Americans each year, I always ask the question:

"What happens to you, a member of the middle class if we allow the banks to double your debt every 3 years, while doubling your savings every 1440 years?" Yes, the banks will own everything and American families like yours will own nothing.

By 2000, the credit card industry was out of control and garnered the most customer complaints of any industry in history.

Many big banks were increasing profits by hitting cardholders with hidden fees, many of which were illegal.

They even went as far as stealing from customers by receiving payments on time, but not posting them until after the due date, so a late fee and permanent hikes on interest rates could be charged. Despite criminal activities and fraudulent business practices, no actual criminal charges were filed against the biggest banks.

We are all of us creatures of habit, accustomed, if not expected to have savings and checking accounts, CDs, a few credit cards, auto loans, and thirty year fixed mortgages. These have become the norms for so many American families, and to be without feels oddly uncomfortable, because ours is a culture of borrowing to buy things we cannot afford.

So using plastic and incurring never-ending debt has become an addiction for many. And as with any addiction, it is incredibly hard to get people to give it up.

Credit cards can do as much damage as cigarettes in their own way (and I am certain my life would have been far better if neither existed). Cigarettes can kill in time but fewer people are using them due to anti-smoking campaigns and commercials. And fortunately, fewer children will become lifelong customers of tobacco simply by "keeping the wolves away from the sheep."

So why are there no big government anti-credit card campaigns? Credit card debt can also kill you in time given the stress caused by debt. In this case, the addicts may be your closest friends and relatives. Some of them are living lives of quiet desperation, drowning in ever-deepening debt. The well-being of any country is tied to the health of its families. The big banks have become financial predators; preying on families for higher profits. If you were to ask big banking executives, "What were you trying to accomplish by sending out tens of millions of credit card applications every month?" I suspect they would answer you as follows: "We were helping American consumers gain more opportunities to fulfill their dreams, build their credit, and thus strengthen the economy."

The opposite is true.

Banks control the credit system. Because we are told we have to use their products to get good credit, they hold the power to continue driving Americans (and the world) further into debt.

To correct the current course and put our country back on track, it is imperative that this power of the credit system be taken from the banks and given back to the hands of the people. In this regard, there has been some progress.

Regulation of the credit card industry has been tried time and time again. Over the years, many bills have been proposed to attempt to stop banks from driving Americans into debt, and to cap fees and interest rates. Bankers pushed and successfully blocked any regulation of the industry. "A ban on marketing credit cards to college students," and "caps on interest rates," were blocked and buried by the banking industry.

But on Monday, February 22nd, 2010, a considerable dent in the harmful practices of the credit card industry took place. This was a long-awaited good day for Americans, and a day of reckoning for the banks. A law went into effect that caused banks to potentially lose billions in profits. Despite the tremendous power of the banking lobby, the CARD Act (Credit Card Accountability Responsibility and Disclosure Act) was passed.

This act includes reforms that will not only prevent banks from marketing to college students, but will make getting a credit card for anyone under the age of 21 illegal without a co-signing parent or guardian. The co-signer will then be liable for any charges on the card and will, therefore, be able to keep tabs on how much and where the young cardholder is spending.

The co-signer will also have complete power to control the credit limit, restricting banks from continuing to offer students larger credit lines once they have them in debt. And pizza, soda, and T-shirts can no longer be given away to induce college students to fill out a credit card application.

Additionally, the new law will force banks to apply any new payments to card balances with the highest interest rates first, so they will no longer be able to bury your low interest debt under your high interest debt where you can't get to it.

Bankers will no longer be able to allow a cardholder to go over their available balance and then charge an over-the-limit fee.

Never again will you be automatically enrolled into over-the-limit protection and charged a fee when you do.

Nor will banks be able to charge multiple fees for each and every transaction that is over the limit.

Credit card companies must now process payments the same day they are received. They are no longer able to hold onto your payments until you're past due and so trigger a late fee.

Bankers can no longer get you in debt at a low interest rate, and then increase your rate to 30% on your entire balance because of one late payment on a different credit card.

The most powerful reform in the CARD Act is one element of financial education. As of February 22nd, 2010, the banks are required to print on all their statements the amount of time it will take to get out of credit card debt— when making the minimum payments.

Although the credit system now has in place some important new laws to protect consumers, the banks still send out millions of credit card applications every month and are doing everything they can to outmaneuver the CARD Act. The public is still painfully in debt, the CARD Act is not retro-active, and there is no reason whatsoever to support the banks and their credit card companies—especially when a credit union can handle all your banking needs.

Perhaps you are beginning to see that big banking does not want financial education available to you, since accurate, truthful financial education would be most destructive to the profits of all the big banks.

Chapter 11

THE TRUTH ABOUT YOUR CREDIT SCORE

*Keep in mind that credit scoring formulas
have one primary purpose: to help lenders gauge
the likelihood you'll default based on how you handle credit.
If you stop using credit or use it in a way the formulas don't like
—using only one card, shutting down a bunch of accounts or maxing
out your cards, even if you then pay them off in full—
your scores could suffer."*

–Liz Weston, MSN Money

The primary fallacy about building your credit score is that it is the solution to all of life's financial problems. The truth is that the process of getting a good credit score may be the cause of your financial problems.

Your parents, who probably have good credit, may have sung the same song about the importance of getting the highest credit score possible.

Nothing is said, (or honestly calculated) about how your parents and grandparents, (who may also have good credit) have paid millions in interest to maintain their high scores. The banks will continue to sell the lie, a lie never challenged, only passed on and cemented as fact.

When a banker goes on and on about the benefits of acquiring good credit, customer beware. Here is the truth of the matter:

If you borrow money from the bank and pay interest, you will qualify to borrow more money and pay more interest to the bank. And, you'll then see your credit score soar. Sounds reasonable, doesn't it?

The next time you hear someone say, "I need good credit," you may want to respond with the same question that I do. I simply ask, "What for?"

Here are a few other questions to consider:

"How much interest has been taken from my family to pay

for auto loans, credit cards, and home mortgages?"

"Where would we be financially if we had invested those interest payments for the benefit of me and my family?"

"If we keep following the bank's counsel of securing good credit, who ultimately benefits?"

Despite new regulatory laws of the CARD Act that keep the banks at bay, I believe that they will, in time, once again gain access to educational institutions across America, seeking to target students to borrow as they have done in the past. They must lock in this future customer base and begin planting the seeds of good credit. Without the seeds, there can be no harvest. And with no harvest, how will your bank keep up with the future demands of Wall Street?

Good credit, from the banker's view, mainly encourages you to buy more things you can't afford, binding you ever more tightly to the banking system.

Millions of houses have been purchased with good credit, only to be lost as consumers are encouraged to borrow more for home furnishings, home improvements and electronics. Credit scores soar for a while, but in time the debt becomes too much. People are forced to refinance more than once, resulting in higher mortgage costs. Foreclosure is then a common scenario.

The goal can be good credit—while never borrowing from

a bank—and paying very little interest, if any, for the rest of your life. And if you must borrow, use a credit union, not a bank (see Chapter 16).

No book about banking would be complete without a brief description of what the banks call revolvers and deadbeats.

The majority of profits for the banks come from those people they call "revolvers." Revolvers, in the credit card industry, are the tens of millions who carry a balance on their cards every month and pay interest to the banks with little reduction to their principal, if any. They simply carry revolving balances.

Every month without fail they line the pockets of banking executives without knowing the actual cost of neglecting their debt. And because of this, revolvers remain on the edge of a financial cliff, and with just one slip, bad credit will be the least of their problems.

Bankers love revolvers. They know that on a balance of $10,000 with a 2%, or $200 minimum payment, and with a 24% interest rate, the cost to the credit card holder alone is $2,400 a year—$200 a month!

This simple formulation shows why all credit companies induce customers to increase their credit lines as much as possible, while reducing minimum payments. This equation can lock customers in debt indefinitely.

Revolvers, what the bankers call their "sweet spot," will never get out from under their burden of debt. What is most disturbing is that many of these revolvers carry enough cash in their savings accounts to reduce large portions of their balances. Some have more than enough to pay off their entire credit card debt, but they don't do it. These revolvers actually borrow their own money back at high interest rates and the bank charges them to do so! Revolvers maintain their savings in the banks, receive little or no interest, but keep making minimum payments on their credit cards, all in the name of having good credit.

"I have great credit because I keep a balance on my credit card," are words revolvers use while getting robbed of their future through endless interest payments to the banks.

Bankers don't want you to know that behind closed doors they have marked you as a revolver because you are a major source of their income. With their sophisticated software, even if you don't want to be a revolver, bankers will continue targeting you with pin-point accuracy to keep you in credit card debt.

Most Americans covet a good credit score, but don't know the factors that drive their scores higher or lower. Your "FICO" is a score tracked by an organization called the Fair Issac Corporation. Your score is what banks look at to determine how much they can charge when you take a loan. Their access to what should be private information about every American who has any sort of credit is daunting. Bankers not only know the exact details of your spending habits, but more importantly, they find it very easy to identify the "revolvers." Ironically, the envelopes in the mail will increase with more credit card applications. Because the lion's share of bank profits comes from revolvers, the banks' goal is to keep them more and more in debt, paying only the minimums. This will, of course, keep many revolvers in debt for life.

On the other hand, banks despise "deadbeats." A deadbeat in the credit card industry is a customer who pays off his entire credit card balance every month. Banks make little or no profit on deadbeats. In many cases banks will lose money on them because of the cost of air miles and rewards, while gaining zero interest from them using the card.

Deadbeats go on luxurious vacations at the expense of the banks by using their cards every month and earning points towards free hotel stays and air miles.

In fact, the hunt for revolvers and avoiding marketing to deadbeats has become a process of analyzing massive amounts of data to determine how and when you spend your money.

If you must carry a credit card, never be a revolver and take full advantage of credit card companies by elevating yourself to the status of "deadbeat."

Saving money and establishing good credit is only bank propaganda with the sole purpose of keeping you entrapped within their debt matrix—where the banks' credit card companies can make or change the rules at will to ensure that they always win—and you always lose.

Chapter 12

THE MORAL DEFICIT OF THE FEDERAL RESERVE

Most Americans have no real understanding of the operation of the international money lenders. The accounts of the Federal Reserve System have never been audited. It operates outside the control of Congress and manipulates the credit of the United States.

–Senator Barry Goldwater

The topic of the Federal Reserve could be the entire content of a book and many have been written about it. In keeping with our theme, however, it is important to know that the Federal Reserve is actually a private bank, and this bank is sanctioned by the US government to print money.

This is not US dollars they are printing, but Federal Reserve Notes. Simply remove any paper money from your wallet. Along with a picture of an American President and the words "THE UNITED STATES OF AMERICA," you will also see "FEDERAL RESERVE NOTE" printed at the top.

There was a time when people actually did not use paper as money. They had actual gold and silver coins. But as you can imagine, carrying large amounts of silver and gold could get a little heavy (and dangerous), so the bankers came up with a solution to solve this problem.

They proposed that all the gold and silver be held in a vault at the bank for safekeeping and they would issue a receipt—a piece of paper designating equal worth. The bankers promised that the receipt could be redeemed at any time for the gold or silver. This paper (now called money) could also be lent out and interest could be charged on the loan.

It was just a matter of time, once the bankers learned that few people ever returned to the bank at the same time to collect their gold or silver, they simply began printing more paper, lending out far more of it than the amount of gold and silver stored in their vaults. The bankers began to accumulate great wealth, stealing millions in interest.

Eventually, the people suspected that there was virtually nothing backing the paper and too many of them arrived at once to collect their gold and silver—and the bank scheme was exposed as entirely fraudulent.

What is most important to understand is that these bankers didn't even receive a slap on the wrist for their crimes. They were, (and continue to be) highly influential within the government that provided them protection from any wrongdoing.

Simply printing numbers on paper and lending it out sounds irrational, doesn't it? But this Monopoly money is exactly what we carry around in our wallets today. Paper backed by nothing.

This paper that we all have been told is money is simply printed and then loaned to Americans as debt. And, as with all debt, these federal bank notes must be paid back with interest.

Loans are secured by the American taxpayer. Today, all of us are forever in debt to this private bank founded in 1913 called the Federal Reserve.

Most Americans are aware that when they swipe their credit card, or sign for a mortgage that they are in debt. But almost all Americans fail to understand that they were already in debt long before they took that loan. They were in debt first to the Federal Reserve.

Today, the heavy financial burden breaking the backs of all taxpayers is only now being scrutinized for the first time in over a hundred years. In 2012, Congress finally passed a bill to audit the Federal Reserve. It amazes me that for more than a century our government, regardless of which party has been in power, has allowed the Fed to print money and has never once been permitted to look into its books.

The question is, how will we ever get out of debt if we persist in borrowing money from this private bank?

The solution is simple: For our country to free itself of this ancient financial burden, congress must vote to eradicate the Federal Reserve and print real American money with public taxpayers having ultimate scrutiny.

It really is that simple.

Chapter 13

WHEN WAS GASOLINE 99 CENTS PER GALLON?

*We are in danger of being overwhelmed with irredeemable paper,
mere paper representing not gold or silver, no sir, representing nothing
but broken promises, bad faith, bankrupt corporations,
cheated creditors and a ruined people."*

**–Daniel Webster,
in a speech to the senate, 1833**

I n 1998 in California, a gallon of gasoline cost 99 cents. The same gallon of gasoline costs about 4 dollars today. That is 400% inflation in just 15 short years.

To the average person, inflation means, "The things that I buy get more expensive over time, right?" This is true, but not the full picture. This definition assumes that your bank has nothing to do with it. The fact of the matter is that banks are the primary cause of much inflation, and the Federal Reserve is the granddaddy of it all. As a consequence, we are getting poorer at an accelerated rate and the banks are to blame.

Inflation, simply put, is printing an excess of money. The more money printed, the more there is to chase the same amount of goods and services, causing prices to rise.

A fundamental question follows: "Why print more money?"

The answer to this lies in an examination of all the ways the world bankers are secretly stealing away the future from all of us.

They do this initially by printing money, which is then logged as debt to the Federal Reserve. This constant printing causes inflation, which results in your money losing its purchasing power. Then, by leveraging and expanding the supply of money (when issuing debt), the biggest banks cause even more inflation.

Let's explore this through a specific example:

What if there was only $100 available to buy all the goods and services in the United States? That $100 would be all there was in circulation to buy all the goods and services in the country. The cost of those goods and services would likely not increase, or increase very slowly. If there were an increase in the volume of money to $200, wouldn't the cost of those goods and services double, as $200 would now be available to chase the same amount of goods and services?

On the current stage, the Federal Reserve with the blessing of Washington, continues to print money, attempting to support social programs and buy votes. And, the banks will continue to leverage that newly printed money, using only bank entries to track the debt.

This will tend to help stimulate the economy by helping millions go deeper in debt, and with a banker's pat on the shoulder, be rewarded with good credit—while simultaneously losing the purchasing power of their money.

You can expect that with each election year the Federal Reserve will turn the presses on high to stimulate the economy and therefore buy more votes.

In the future, your paper money may realize its true value and become worthless. Remember, it does not matter if you have a dollar in your wallet—it only matters what that dollar can buy. If you have a dollar in a savings account growing at .05% rate of return and inflation is at 4%, the purchasing power of your one dollar is declining by 3.95% a year.

It is indeed a losing battle.

Chapter 14

WASHINGTON BUSTED

*I do not think it is an exaggeration to say history
is largely a history of inflation, usually inflations engineered by
governments for the gain of governments.*

**–Friedrich Hayek,
Nobel Prize winning economist**

I f you were fortunate enough to attend a business or economics class, you may have been told that the average, long-term inflation rate is 3%. Although this is the government's commonly stated rate, there is a big fly in the ointment.

Have you ever noticed that the things you buy are increasing in price more than 3% every year? I certainly have, but who am I to argue with the government? I'm simply the son of a bricklayer. All kidding aside, the fact of the matter is that 3% inflation represents a half truth. It involves a similar strategy some use in the calculation of their taxes—a bit of creative accounting.

Let's say, for the sake of exercise, a fellow by the name of Phil earns $100,000 of income his first year. Of course, Phil reports this to the tax man.

The next year Phil earns $200,000, but he only reports $100,000 of income. With a little creative accounting, his explanation to the tax man is as follows: "I worked twice as hard the second year. Therefore, I didn't actually earn twice the income." He would hope that on hearing this completely reasonable explanation, the IRS would say, "That makes sense," and allow Phil on his way. But we know the absurdity of this ploy. The IRS would throw Phil in jail for his "creativity."

But the government uses all forms of similar creative accounting to hide the true rate of inflation from the public, especially after the inflation peak of 1980.

U.S. Annual Inflation Rate

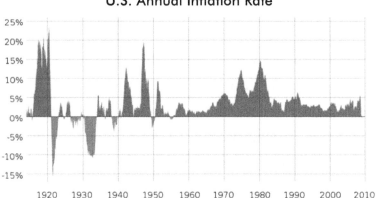

What is not commonly known is that the government in 1980 removed food and energy from the publicly stated inflation rate.

You could be asking, "Why would the government report a blatantly false inflation rate to the American public?"

The answer is disturbing.

The government consistently promises to keep America's pensions, Social Security, Medicare, Medicaid, government salaries, and other entitlement programs adjusted for inflation. So rather than pay what is owed, simply lying about the inflation rate is a more feasible solution.

If the Bureau of Labor Statistics (the BLS) were allowed to report the real inflation rate, the government would be at risk of going broke. Rather than deal with that eventuality, the government manipulates and devises its own formula to calculate inflation. The alternative of raising taxes and laying off of government workers would be immensely unpopular and would certainly result in the loss of votes.

"And how does all this relate to banking?" you may be asking.

Consider this: if the government were to report the actual inflation rate, it would then need to adjust all the costs of pensions, Social Security benefits, government salaries, and other entitlement programs to the non-manipulated rate.

Where would they get the money to do that?

By printing it.

Just imagine for a moment if the Federal Reserve simply printed more money to keep up with rising inflation and the banks leveraged that money into debt—it would cause even more inflation.

The faster the inflation, the more the government will have to pay out to adjust for it, and the more money it would need to print.

This vicious cycle, once started, is very hard to stop, like an expanding snowball rolling down a hill. As Washington and the Federal Reserve continue to run the presses, the snowball becomes unstoppable, forever gaining momentum and size.

How do most people contribute to the cycle? Every dollar saved in a bank account or borrowed on a credit card adds more volume to the snowball.

So getting out of debt and never saving in a bank again will have a far more positive impact on the future of this country than most think. The result of leaving banking forever is that the bankers of the world would become poorer as more Americans become financially free.

Now we are primed to see how the banks' and government's financial manipulations bring this vicious cycle into existence and how all of us are affected.

Our government, under the heels of the bankers, promotes spending, not saving and investing. The health of our country is gauged with polling agencies such as the "Consumer Confidence Survey," which measures spending trends. If we spend more, they say we are more "confident" and celebrate our increased spending, and then tell us that our economy is thriving. The fact of the matter is, people are spending money they do not have, falling into even greater debt.

It is obvious that the stability of our country would be based upon saving and not spending what we do not have. Unfortunately, paying down our debt is regarded as an economy in decline.

The banks are determined to maintain the financial

ignorance of the American people and consistently derail the health of our economy.

Our founding fathers would not approve of the direction of our country, the size and control of the government, the level of taxation levied against its people, and certainly not the power of big corporations to influence the laws.

Capitalism itself is not being practiced by Wall Street. It is thievery and greed masked as capitalism, currently under the protection of a government growing in size. There is no competition, and the best the banks have to offer has resulted in slavery to millions and a downward spiral of financial chaos.

Winston Churchill once humorously said: "The inherent vice of capitalism is the unequal sharing of blessings; the inherent virture of socialism is the equal sharing of miseries."

Our government's allowing the practice of fractional reserve banking to continue will keep you and your family in constant debt, borrowing money that does not exist, and ultimately results in the loss of your purchasing power.

We must start a grass roots revolution and close all our bank savings and CD accounts, and refinance all our debt to local credit unions. And perhaps one day, as Abraham Lincoln had hoped, take our country back from the banks.

Chapter 15

SOCIAL SECURITY ON THE CUTTING BOARD

*Without changes, in 2033 the Social Security Trust Fund
will be able to pay only about 77¢ for each dollar of scheduled benefits.*

–Your Social Security Statement

A s with all Ponzi schemes, Social Security may be the grandest of them all. And the ultimate destiny of all Ponzi schemes is their ultimate collapse.

When I was a teenager, my mother called me "Money Mark." I was intent on becoming wealthy and remember well my very first attempt at securing my financial freedom while only in my teens. I received this letter offering me a huge return on my money. I was very excited. All I had to do was buy a list of names and addresses from a company, send dollar bills in the mail, and within a matter of months I'd be a millionaire as tens of thousands of people would be sending me dollar bills in the mail. I would be wealthy in my early teens!

There were all kinds of true stories of people who received $100,000 or more, simply from buying a list and sending their money in the mail. It was only a matter of time. And so every afternoon I checked the mail, expecting my first onslaught of envelopes, which of course, never came.

What did I know of pyramid schemes? But I was not deterred as I was "Money Mark" and I was young, resilient, and not to be discouraged. Through the Internet, I found a second opportunity that was rock solid; a small international start-up company that had great potential for high rates of return. They were looking for a few smart investors to provide "seed money" to get them up and running, so I sent a check in the mail to put my money hard at work for me.

I think you can guess the end of the story. I learned several valuable lessons and some rules for investing:

First, I learned that there is no such thing as get-rich-quick.

Second, I learned what pyramid schemes were, and more importantly, not to invest in them.

Third, I learned what Ponzi schemes were and not to invest in them either.

The originator of the scheme was Charles Ponzi, so infamous for his con they named the whole thing after him.

After World War I, Ponzi promised clients a 50% profit within 45 days, or 100% profit within 90 days by buying discounted postal reply coupons from other countries and redeeming them at face value in the United States. When word got out that a few initial investors were making money as promised, thousands more bought in. Ponzi paid first-time investors money from the new people while keeping most of it for himself.

Only one other man in history has made the term, "Ponzi scheme" more famous than the originator—Bernie Madoff, currently serving one hundred and fifty years in prison for his sixty-five billion dollar con. He even cheated his own sister and "made-off" with a reported three million of her savings.

Ponzi schemes work roughly like this:

First, money is taken from initial investors (like me as a teen) who are promised a high rate of return on their investment. When these investors begin receiving profits from the organization, they begin to tell others of the great rate of return on their money. What the first time clients do not know is that their profits do not come from legitimate investments, but from new cash pouring in from new people buying in. Eventually the scheme collapses as investors become suspicious and too many arrive at the same time to remove their money.

And that is the key to identify Ponzi schemes: If too many investors show up at the same time to remove their money, and there is not enough to pay all the investors, you have a Ponzi scheme.

Now that you understand the inner workings of Ponzi schemes, the question arises: Is the Social Security Administration in the same camp?

Every paycheck across America is issued only after federal taxes, state taxes, and a hefty deduction to fund FICA, (the Federal Insurance Contribution Act) established to pay for Medicare and Social Security.

Many people beginning to pay into the Social Security system today will never see any of their money in their retirement. It is almost certain that this primary historic entitlement program may be lost to future generations, and it is best that we prepare ourselves for alternatives.

Business owners and the wealthy know that the Social Security system is nothing more than a giant Ponzi scheme and they don't expect any money in return for their investment.

They know that if too many investors show up to get their money at the same time and there is not enough to pay them, they have invested in a Ponzi scheme.

There are 80,000,000 baby boomers out there, 11,000 of them turning 65 every day and will continue to do so until the year 2029. The United States is in a massive debt crisis, owing trillions to Social Security for aging beneficiaries, as well as huge sums for other entitlement programs such as Medicaid and Medicare. Americans have trustingly invested every month in FICA payments—investing in a government sanctioned Ponzi scheme.

To manage our monumental debt, the government is not only borrowing from the fund, but must also print more and more money to keep up with the rising payments on debts to the Federal Reserve (and China). Ultimately, the dollar is at risk of becoming worthless, and the entire system, as with all Ponzi schemes, will collapse.

There are no exceptions; it is simply a matter of time.

It is very important that you upgrade your financial IQ,

learn how to grow your money away from the banks, and keep it working for you in a tax-free environment, as your own personal savings is the only money you can count on, if you ever plan to retire.

Remember two simple rules as you travel down the path toward financial independence:

Rule #1: You must keep your money from the banks.

Rule #2: You must (legally) keep your money from the government.

PART TWO

BANKS NO MORE

Chapter 16

CREDIT UNIONS: OWN YOUR BANK

A credit union is not an ordinary financial concern, seeking to enrich its members. Neither is it a loan banking company, seeking to make a profit at the expense of the unfortunates. The credit union is nothing of the kind; it is the expression in the field of economics of a high social ideal."

**Alphonse Desjardins,
Founder of Caisses Populaires Desjardins
(the "peoples bank" or credit union),
1854 to 1920**

Many of my clients aren't quite sure what a credit union actually is. If asked, they often say, "They're just smaller banks and I don't think I qualify to join one."

On both counts, they're quite mistaken.

The following definition of what a credit union is will serve us well:

"A not-for-profit financial institution that is owned and operated entirely by its members."

Credit unions provide financial services for their members, including savings and lending. Large organizations and companies may set up credit unions for their members and employees respectively. To join a credit union, a person must ordinarily belong to a participating organization such as a college alumni association or labor union. But many credit unions today only require that you live, work, worship, attend school in the area, or be a relative of a current member. When a person deposits money, he or she becomes a member and owner of the credit union, because their deposits grant them partial ownership.

A New York Times article on February 9th, 2010, titled "The Least-Trusted Banks in America," stated:

"Customers of the biggest banks in the United States are the least likely to believe their financial institution does what's best for them as opposed to what's best for the bottom line, according to a new report from Forrester Research."

According to the article, about 70% of Americans believe that their banks will make decisions based on profits, rather than what is good for their customers. On the contrary, the survey finds that customers of credit unions believe that their organizations make decisions on the basis of what is best for them, about 70% of the time.

Fortunately, and quite recently, many credit unions do not require people to have special status to join, other than living in the area, and many only require a small membership fee, such as $10, and often the $10 goes to charity.

According to the World Council of Credit Unions, there are more than 200 million members worldwide. And just within North America (as of 2012), there are more than 7,794 credit unions with more than 109,000,000 members.

In 2008, many Americans went to their savings and CDs, only to find they were only insured up to $100,000. For many who worked their entire lives with savings of $250,000 held in CDs, and expecting 100% safety and security from the bank, they could very well lose as much as $150,000.

Remember, bankers don't really keep your money in their vault. They keep it working for them in speculative investments and might very well lose it. If there were another economic crisis as seen in 2008 and too many customers came at once to withdraw their money, only a fraction of it would be there.

Fortunately, credit unions are not engaged in the practice of fractional reserve banking. Moreover, the vast majority (about 98%) are "Federal" credit unions—insured by the National Credit Union Share Insurance Fund which is backed by the full faith and credit of the US Government. In addition, because credit unions do not invest speculatively, the risk of default on your money is considerably lessened. In fact, not one penny of insured savings has ever been lost by a member of a federally insured credit union.

In reality, most of us do currently need some sort of institution for day-to-day financial transactions: to deposit paychecks, access our money, secure car loans, and home mortgages. The far better alternative to a bank is a credit union.

At credit unions you will generally not be encouraged to get multiple credit cards.

They pay higher interest rates on savings accounts and CDs than a bank.

They have never received a bail-out at the expense of taxpayers.

They have a larger network of ATMs; therefore you will have better access to your money without fees.

Years ago, I was in a bind and needed to borrow a few hundred dollars from my credit card. I had a bank-issued card at that time. They not only charged me a 5% transaction fee, but also penalized me with a 29.99% interest rate to help me out in my emergency. This experience hit home and I learned an important lesson: Bankers kick the hardest when you're down and already financially bleeding.

Today, as a customer of a credit union, I can take a cash advance from my credit union issued credit card with no transaction fees and a 10% fixed interest rate. Now, I may not need to do this, but it is nice to know that my credit union will not be the one to kick me in an emergency if I need the help.

I have even advised many of my clients to take a loan out against the equity of their car to pay off 24% interest credit card debt. Borrowing at 2-4% from the equity of your car to pay down 24% interest debt can save a fortune in interest— and propel you out of debt while making the same payments.

Most Americans don't like or trust their banks for good reasons but often don't know where else to go. They settle for the convenience of multiple branches of the mega banks, as well as having access to their money at thousands of ATMs, despite getting charged at competing bank's machines.

The fact is credit unions are far more effective on both counts. Throughout the United States, they offer the best access to your cash without any fees. The majority of credit unions are part of a nationwide network called the CO-OP Network. And through this network you may never pay an ATM fee again to get access to your money. You can withdraw your money across the United States (and Canada) without paying a fee. How?

Go to the website of your local credit union and search for the CO-OP Network logo:

My own credit union states the following:

"Welcome to the CO-OP, the largest credit union-only ATM Network in the country. As a member of a CO-OP Network credit union, your ATM card provides you with surcharge-free access to 30,000 ATMs nationwide. This includes 9,000 deposit-taking ATMs and 5,500 7-Eleven locations throughout the U.S. & Canada."

As the slogan goes, "Oh, thank heaven for 7-Eleven," for helping me get access to my cash without being robbed by a banker.

Remember, only CO-OP Network ATMs guarantee you surcharge-free access to your money.

There is a 7-Eleven or credit union ATM on almost every corner, but only if you are with a credit union. You can also get your cash at Costco and Walgreens through the same network, and they are adding more ATMs all the time. The same cannot be said for your bank. In fact banks will claim that they are convenient because they have more ATMs. This is simply not the case.

As of the writing of this book, the biggest of the mega banks has approximately 16,200 ATMs across the country, whereas the credit union network has more than 30,000 FEE-FREE ATMs, including machines at 7-Eleven, Walgreens, and Costco.

You can even use your mobile phone to find an ATM location with no fees. Simply send a text to MYCOOP (692667) from your cell phone. In the body of the text enter an address (with city and state), zip code, or intersection. In about 30 seconds, the service will reply with the CO-OP Network surcharge-free ATM nearest to your location.

Download an APP on your mobile phone by searching "COOP ATM." This application will give you an even simpler way of locating network ATMs.

Go to www.movecu.com and conduct a search to find credit unions in your area.

Use your credit union account for paying bills and

managing short term expenses. Talk with your credit union about refinancing all bank-debt you have, which can lower your interest rates dramatically. Credit unions have on average much lower rates on auto loans and credit cards. Then focus on eliminating your credit card debt entirely.

Join the credit union revolution by sharing this book with three friends or family members, inspiring them to close their bank accounts and find a credit union.

Shop around and explore several local credit unions to find the best rates, access to business services (if needed), the best service, friendly staff, and the best overall experience. Even keep the credit unions competing for your business.

Chapter 17

FINANCIAL ADVISORS

My two rules of investing: Rule one – never lose money.
Rule two – never forget rule one.

–Warren Buffett

There are financial advisors out there who will give you honest advice—not for his or her benefit, but for yours. Ask questions and seek the one who will patiently answer. As you go forward in establishing a relationship with an advisor, remember that your financial education is as vital as how you invest your money.

Be wary of someone who will only say, "Trust me, I know what I'm doing."

There are many types of advisors who like to use the term "financial advisor" to describe what they do. Some of these are actually not financial advisors at all and many represent the interests of the company they work for, and not yours.

Here are the five types: bank advisors, "captive" advisors, insurance salesmen, stockbrokers, and independent advisors.

Many bank advisors have minimum investment requirements in the tens of thousands before they are encouraged to help you. Their agenda is to maintain quotas and they may not have an incentive to build long-term wealth for their clients. Many represent mutual funds of the companies they work for to maximize profits to shareholders.

"Captive" advisors only sell financial investment products of the companies they work for. They will convince you that their opportunities are the very best, but it is imperative that you have access to more than they can offer—as their products may be inferior to what is available in the marketplace. They have bills to pay and must sell, sell, sell to keep current on their debt payments.

Insurance salesmen are only licensed to sell insurance-based products, and many sell low interest-bearing "whole life" policies earning 3 to 4% guaranteed return, with the supposed advantages of insurance for tax-deferred growth. But how are these investments safe and secure if earning only 3 or 4%, when inflation is 4%? The truth is that you're guaranteed to make nothing on your money with many of these insurance products when factoring in inflation. And, when an insurance company gives you a low rate of return, they are using your money to invest at higher rates for themselves, much like a bank.

Insurance agents may often neglect to tell you that if you borrow money from your investment policy, you will be charged 8%, even though you're only earning around 4%. Charging you 8% while paying you 4%, seems almost as shady as the lies that so freely fall off the tongues of Wall Street bankers.

Great stock brokers are now few and far between and many only work with highly-educated investors with a high net worth. You may be the kind of person who has opened up an online investment account to buy a few stocks to "test the waters." Chances are you've made and lost some money, which can be an important part of upgrading your financial IQ. If you decide to pick stocks yourself, be sure not to experiment with money you can't afford to lose.

Independent advisors are generally self-employed and own their own business. What makes them "independent" is that they are not captive to a specific company or product. This could be the best choice as they can have access to vast investment choices, and have a long term interest in helping you build your wealth.

Keep in mind, just because they call themselves "independent" does not mean they are all competent. Many advisors simply don't know the difference between a good and bad mutual fund. I know this because over the years I've reviewed hundreds of plans from financial professionals (independent, insurance salesmen, captive agents, and bank advisors), and have found that many investment accounts are loaded with poor quality mutual funds—funds that actually perform worse than the stock market.

Many credit unions provide independent advisors that have the best interest of their members at heart. They generally don't have quotas and credit unions don't promote their own mutual funds, so they have no loyalty to a specific bank or company. As credit unions are not-for-profit, they will not refer you back to the teller for "an introductory 0%

credit card as a preferred customer."

Working with an advisor can keep your investments completely bank-free and potentially tax-free as well.

In the following chapter, we will cover how to review your investments, determine what options are best for you, and how they are taxed.

Chapter 18

SAVING SHORT, MID AND LONG TERM

In the long run, it's not just how much money you make that will determine your future prosperity. It's how much of that money you put to work by saving and investing it.

—Peter Lynch

People in this country purchased more wine and coffee than gold in the year 2000. They were buying "commodities," just the wrong ones. It is my belief that if you can buy wine or coffee, you can invest. And with some help from a good advisor, you can even learn to make money with rising commodity prices.

The goals of investing are threefold: to create a short term emergency fund to cover expenses for a minimum of six to twelve months in the event of a lay-off or illness; as well as investing mid-term for big-ticket items like houses, cars, or college funds; and long term for the purpose of your retirement.

For the short term, keep at least six months of emergency reserves in your credit union accounts for unexpected expenses.

For mid-term investing, you can then talk with your advisor about the options for investing in a number of mutual funds—where the growth can be taxed at rates lower than ordinary savings accounts.

There are literally thousands of mutual funds and as many financial advisors touting them. So how can you know where to go or what to invest in? In addition to many years working with clients, I have discovered some effective tools to identify the very best funds.

First you must know what a "ticker" is. A ticker is simply an arrangement of letters that represent a company. For example, if seeking the price of Microsoft, the ticker is MSFT. If looking for the price of Google, search for GOOG and you can find the current price. Almost all mutual funds you now own or buy in the future will have a ticker, which will help you determine how your funds have been performing. This may also reflect the competence of your advisor, whether they are really working for the bank, captive, or independent.

Thankfully, there is a powerful resource that can give you an indication of how a particular fund is performing in relation to all the other funds of a similar type. Check out www.morningstar.com.

Pick out a ticker from your statement or simply type in the name of an investment you own where it says "Quote." Throughout the site you will discover various reports with your mutual fund's historical performance over the last three, five, and ten years, degrees of risk, rates of return, and other factors. The language is wonderfully easy to understand. Morningstar rates mutual funds and many investments with a simple rating of one ★ to five ★ ★ ★ ★ ★.

If you find a one or two star fund in your portfolio, it is time to seriously ask some questions about who is giving you financial advice. One star means the "professional" money manager of the fund is performing worse than 90% of the others who manage similar funds.

Start investing with $50 a month if that is all you can afford. What is most important is to develop the habit of saving. Your advisor will know of mutual fund companies that can start you off with minimal amounts. It's a small step but a step in the direction toward financial security.

For the long term, there are different scenarios:

If you're an employee, your company may make automatic withdrawals from your paycheck to fund a 401(k) on your behalf. These "qualified plans" require that you contribute before-tax dollars. They are not taxable until you withdraw your money at retirement. At that time, you will be paying regular income taxes on your withdrawals.

Fortunately, matching contributions (if any) from the company you work for can really help your money grow and help alleviate the pain of the taxation on the backend. If you have the option of a matching contribution on your 401(k), be sure to contribute up to the full match available, but also check into the performance of your plan to be sure you are using the best options.

If you are self-employed, there will be no options for a matching contribution as within a 401(k); therefore, I suggest you use a combination of the following to bring you tax-free gains at retirement.

Roth IRAs: In this case, you invest with after tax dollars, to benefit from tax-free gains and tax-free distributions. Think of it this way: A farmer has a basket of seeds. Would you rather pay tax on the seeds or the harvest? For most Americans, it is best to pay tax on the initial contribution, or the "seed," rather than the amassed amount at retirement, the "harvest." Again, with a Roth IRA, you will never be taxed on the gains or the income at retirement.

Cash accumulation within life insurance policies: There are unique insurance policies that can also be used as tax shelters and wealth transfer strategies. The biggest problem with these policies is not the policies themselves but the agents who sell them. Many times, these agents are "captive" to one company, which can severely limit their ability to offer you the best policy. If you would like to learn more about this strategy, pick up a copy of "The Retirement Miracle" by Patrick Kelly.

So let's lay out a plan for growing and protecting your money while keeping it out of the grasp of the banks.

The Ten-Step Plan in the next chapter will put you directly on the path to financial independence.

Chapter 19

TEN-STEP PLAN FOR FINANCIAL SECURITY

Another way to solve the traffic problems of the country is to pass a law that only paid-for cars be allowed to use the highways.

–Will Rogers

Follow this plan closely and you will build a solid financial foundation for your future.

By teaching this plan to your brothers and sisters, nieces and nephews, cousins, aunts, and uncles, you may change the financial legacy of your family forever.

Teach this plan to your neighbors and friends and so improve the stability of your local neighborhoods. Watch as families stabilize and divorce rates plummet.

Teach this plan at work and watch productivity increases as your colleagues get out of debt, become more optimistic and, in doing so, actually improve your company's financial future.

Teach this plan to your church, synagogue, and mosque members, and watch as your spiritual community begins to prosper and become free of debt.

Teach this plan to your children at home and in their schools, and thus plant the seeds for a bank free, debt free future generation.

1. No more bank-issued credit cards

Call 1-888-5-OPTOUT (1-888-567-8688) and stop receiving any pre-approved credit card offers in the mail. This will also protect you from having the banks sell your information to other banks and credit companies.

2. Cut up all your bank-issued credit cards

Slice up those department and home improvement store

cards too as they usually have the highest interest rates and fees. If you absolutely feel you must have a credit card, apply for one with a $5-10,000 credit limit from your credit union. Use it only in emergencies and pay the full balance each month.

3. Live debt-free

Set a goal to never accumulate debt outside of your mortgage. Rather than purchase big ticket items on credit, save money in mutual funds until you have enough for that new car, furniture, or flat screen TV. This may mean living more frugally, but spending more than you have ensures a lifetime of debt and unhappiness.

4. Find a credit union

Shop around. There's a friendly place just around the corner that can mean a positive, lifelong relationship. You now know the advantages and the inherent values. Joining a credit union is not just a smart financial decision but is also a distinctly moral choice. Maintain a credit union checking account for your day-to-day expenditures as well as a savings account for emergencies.

Your credit union will offer you much better rates on:

Car loans

Credit cards (if you need one)

Refinancing of debt with few or no fees.

Once all this is in place:

5. Fire your bank!

Close all your saving and checking accounts. Release your money from bank CDs in search of higher returns. Even with a small penalty, you may gain from the higher savings rates at your credit union—and by investing in mutual funds. You can really get your money working hard for you each day. Be sure to set up your accounts at the credit union first, so the transition out of the bank is smooth and efficient.

6. Retain a good, independent financial advisor

Make sure that whoever you choose is there to represent you...an intelligent, creative person who has high integrity and ethics. Good advisors understand the primary importance of saving in wealth-building strategies. They can keep all your money working for you every hour of every day.

7. Set up short-term and mid-term savings

Keep three to six months of emergency reserves in the credit union in case of unexpected expenses.

For mid-term savings, look into investing into high-yielding mutual funds. There are numerous funds out there that have ten year histories of earning 6% or higher, which can potentially—using The Rule of "72"—double your money in 12 years.

8. Long-term retirement funds

As discussed in the previous chapter, there are both

qualified plans (such as 401(k)s and IRAs), and non-qualified plans (such as Roth IRAs) that your financial advisor can assist you with.

9. Review your mortgage

Talk to your credit union to access the lowest possible rate, and if you can afford it, consider a 15 year fixed loan to accelerate the payoff. If you can't afford the larger payment, look into making bi-weekly mortgage payments on a 30 year loan. For example, if your payment is $1800 per month, send in $900 every two weeks. This simple strategy can pay off a 30 year mortgage in about 25 years (or less), and save you a small fortune in interest.

Your primary goal is to have no debt whatsoever outside of your mortgage, and then, as soon as possible, have no debt at all.

10. Register at www.richmanpoorbank.com

Register your email and get regular updates to access other financial tools that will help you become debt free and clear about your path to financial independence.

11. (Optional) Become a "deadbeat"

This final step is not recommended for everyone and should only be considered by those who understand banking and have a very high financial IQ, combined with great financial discipline. To officially earn the status of deadbeat you may decide to get an additional card from a bank to accumulate air miles, but if you do, and this is the key: make sure to pay off your entire balance in full every month. To recap, a deadbeat is someone who uses their credit cards to take advantage of the banking system by earning air miles and rewards—while paying no interest whatsoever to the banks.

If you implement all of the ten steps, it is my promise to you that you will never again set foot into the trap of the "debt matrix," and you may soon find yourself breathing the pure air of financial independence.

Chapter 20

JACK AND ELLEN: PEACE OF MIND

He looks the whole world in the face for he owes not any man.

–Henry Wadsworth Longfellow

Jack and Ellen arrived at my office at 2 PM on a sunny Wednesday afternoon. With their gifts of coffee and biscotti in hand, they seemed very excited to get things started.

"We both read and reread your manuscript, Mark," said Ellen.

"One word comes to my mind," continued Jack, "Shocking."

"An eye opener would be an understatement. What a wake-up call," said Ellen.

"We've already opened up accounts at our local credit union," said Jack.

"And fired our big bank!" finished Ellen.

We all laughed. "Congratulations!" I said.

"We cut up our credit cards, called the opt-out number, and are looking forward to never receiving another credit card offer in the mail again," Jack said.

"I'm delighted. Of the ten steps to financial security, you're already done with one, two, four, and five."

Remind me then, what's step three?" asked Jack.

"To set goals for living debt free."

A short pause ensued.

"I guess we'll just have to chip away at our debt over the years. I suppose eventually we'll dig ourselves out of the hole we've dug ourselves into," sighed Ellen.

"You have achieved step six, Ellen. You've found yourselves a great advisor," I said as I smiled.

Ellen looked at me woefully. "Is there anything you can do?"

"I've come up with a few recommendations you may find useful." I handed them both a single page with the core details of the plan I prepared for them.

"We're all ears," said Jack.

"Aside from your mortgage, you have $22,385 in credit card debt averaging 20% interest, making payments of around $750 a month. The good news is that Ellen's Prius is paid off and it's worth about $20,000. I suggest that you borrow $20,000 from your credit union, secured by the equity of your car, to pay off your high-interest credit card debt. Both your cars are new enough with fairly low mileage so you should qualify for the loan. Apply the $20,000 loan from the credit union to your credit cards. Given your work histories and great credit, I believe you'll be able to secure this loan and save $325 in interest each month."

"Really?" asked Ellen.

"Yes," I answered. "I suggest that you pay all your highest interest credit card debt with this very low interest auto loan from the credit union. You will have $2,385 in credit card debt remaining but that can be paid off with only a small portion of your savings.

"The next step is to refinance your auto loan on Jack's car at the credit union and reduce the interest rate. On a three-year loan, I estimate your payment will be $286, reduced from $465 per month.

"You will still be carrying an auto loan of $20,000 on Ellen's Prius, but with the lower interest rate, on a 5 year loan, your overall payment will be about $350 a month and, most importantly, we will have eliminated your high-interest credit card debt. I estimate that in about five years, outside of your mortgage, you'll be debt free."

I then added, "If you add everything up from reducing interest rates and payments, you will have freed up about $579 each month.

"A savings of $579 a month! You have no idea what this will mean for us, Mark." Ellen's voice revealed how moved she was.

She continued, "And we can put the $7,200 from the CDs at the bank into some great mutual funds to grow until the kids are ready for college."

"We're not done yet, Ellen. Shall we have a discussion on steps seven and eight?"

"We should keep $15,000 on deposit in a savings account

at the credit union for immediate emergencies, right?" Jack asked.

"Perfect," I said, "that's a great start on step seven which, as you'll recall, is set up to cover six months income in the event of illness, a lay off—unexpected events like that.

"You have about $20,000 in savings and CDs which I suggest you move to the credit union after you pay off the remaining credit card debt. You will then be completely free of high interest debt. How does that sound?"

Ellen smiled, "I wish we would have met you five or ten years ago. Having no credit card debt will feel incredible."

"I agree," Jack said.

"But remember—you don't have to keep all your savings sitting idle at the credit union. Even at that institution, which as you know I admire, your money is not growing there as it can. So I am recommending that you move about $8,800 into highly conservative mutual funds. They have respectable historical rates of return in the neighborhood of 6%, which could be taxed at rates much less than savings accounts."

"That's a heck of a lot better than .05% at the banks!"

"Exactly. Using the 'Rule of 72,' your money has the potential of doubling every twelve years. And if you continue making monthly contributions of $200 as you have been doing at the bank, you have a very real chance of building very large reserves.

"So if you stick with the program and if history repeats itself, your mutual fund savings alone could be worth around $60,000 in just twelve years. Plus, your money that was once sitting idle in the bank will have earned close to $22,000. That's money working hard for you rather than working hard for your bank. And remember, whatever you need from your mutual funds can be electronically transferred without fees to your credit union account within three business days.

"You see Jack, many people believe they're paying themselves first when saving money in their bank, but the reality is they're paying their bank first, not themselves."

"I can see that now," said Ellen. She was entirely focused on the print-out I'd given her. "So shall we move on to our retirement goals?"

"Absolutely, but do you have any questions thus far?"

Neither did, so I went on. "Jack, when you retire, you will have to pay regular income tax on all of your IRA distributions, so I suggest you stop any further contributions, and redirect the money into a Roth IRA. If making a contribution of $5,500 each year earning 10% interest, your investment will grow to well over $1,000,000 when you retire. And remember, Roth IRAs provide tax-free retirement income."

"That sounds fantastic," Jack said, "but what about Ellen's 401(k)?"

"Do you know what the matching contribution is at the hospital on your plan, Ellen?

"Yes, I do. I believe they match dollar for dollar up to the first 3%. Do you suggest I keep it at that rate?"

"Yes I do, Ellen, as that match can really help grow your retirement nest egg. But we can also explore contributing to a Roth IRA for you as well, while you continue to eliminate debt. Unfortunately, many Americans contribute all their retirement money into 401(k)s and IRAs, making Uncle Sam their life-long business partner.

"And Ellen, I also suggest we review the options available in your 401(k) plan to make sure you are choosing the best investments of the funds available."

"No problem," said Ellen, "We can review that from my latest statement."

"Now, no financial plan is complete without reviewing your options for life insurance, and currently Jack's 30 year term policy will terminate at age 58. So I suggest you supplement your term policy with permanent insurance with a $250,000 death benefit. This type of policy is called Index Universal Life insurance, or IUL. Not only will this provide you with insurance for the rest of your life, but if you overfund it, it can also be used to provide additional tax-free retirement income. As I mentioned, it is very important to find an agent who will represent your best interests when it comes to permanent insurance, as many are limited to poor quality policies known as 'whole life' insurance. And many of those agents are captive to the companies they work for.

"I personally contribute to an IUL, as well as a policy called a Variable Universal Life, or VUL. A variable policy simply means that I can pick the mutual funds I invest in. And with the right investment options, I can benefit from strong growth within my policy, while not having to pay taxes as my money grows."

"Incredible," said Ellen.

"My clients are going to love this," added Jack. "I'm thinking that now that we have the extra cash flow, I can max out my Roth IRA and even start an IUL."

"That is exactly what I am suggesting," I said. "And one more thing about IULs: the money accumulated inside your policy is guaranteed against loss, not like in 401(k)s, IRAs, or Roth IRAs. You have everything to gain and nothing to lose."

"How come I've never heard of this?" asked Ellen.

"The wealthy are very much aware of it because they can't use Roth IRAs due to income restrictions. They therefore use insurance to shelter their money from taxes. An IUL policy isn't for everybody but I believe it is suitable for you."

I explained some of the other details of the policy: costs, surrender charges, guarantees, and other benefits. Both Jack and Ellen were impressed.

"And we've already registered our names on your website to keep learning more about how to manage our money," Ellen commented, "so step 9 is done."

"It's now time to talk about step 10—your mortgage: a 30-year fixed loan from your bank. You are paying $3,350 per month with 19 years left on it. Given current mortgage rates and your near perfect credit scores, you're paying far too much in interest." I performed a simple calculation.

"You have $391,000 left and are paying $2,000 per month in interest alone. Frankly, I believe the credit union can also refinance your mortgage and reduce your interest rate. By refinancing your home to a 15 year fixed mortgage, we can likely save you close to $1,000 a month in interest. Not only will your payment drop, you will pay your home off even faster.

"If combining the $400 saved from getting rid of high interest credit card debt, $179 from reducing the interest rate on Jack's auto loan, and the smaller payment on your mortgage, you will have about $1,000 in extra cash flow every month.

"We've been in your office for thirty-five minutes and you've just saved us more than $12,000 a year in interest, and

$1,000 a month in extra cash flow. Mark...you have no idea what this will mean for us." Ellen was holding back tears. Jack put his arm around her. "We have a plan now, direction, after so many years of struggling with debt. And no more sleepless nights."

"My pleasure, Jack, Ellen. Truly." And I meant it. "We'll get together a couple of more times. There is paperwork, applications to fill out, phone calls, and meetings with your credit union, and maybe a call to your 401(k) company, but I believe that by the end of the month we'll have everything taken care of."

Jack and Ellen got up. It looked as if a great weight had been taken from their shoulders. They thanked me more than once, and left.

My coffee was still warm. I cleared my desk, sat back in my chair, and contemplated my own journey getting out of debt and all the mistakes I had made while taking advice from banks. It sure would have been nice if someone had guided me in the right direction—away from banks many years ago.

Chapter 21

IN CONCLUSION

*Many people make the mistake of thinking that
all the challenges in their lives would dissipate if they just had
enough money. Nothing could be further from the truth. Earning more
money, in and of itself, rarely frees people. It's equally ridiculous to
tell yourself that greater financial freedom and mastery of your
finances would not offer you greater opportunities
to expand, share, and create value
for yourself and others.*

–Anthony Robbins

When the mega banks were collapsing in 2008 and 2009, the government bailed them out in the name of saving jobs and protecting the economy from a major depression. The banks were very grateful as record profits were made shortly after the bailouts. They promised the American people that they would free up credit and loans, but the opposite happened. What they did do was lay-off thousands and began increasing interest rates on credit cards, regardless of people's credit rating or history.

Banks obviously feel that they are invincible, believing that the public is powerless to do anything against them. And this has been the case in the past, with many of our elected officials having been advisors to the biggest banks.

It would take incredible courage for our president (whoever that may be when you read this book), to lead Americans with a message to "Stop spending what you don't have and get out of debt." But how could this advice come from a government that spends billions it does not have?

Because the government is unlikely to inspire this imperative shift in the mindset of how we manage money, the responsibility to become debt free and to secure financial independence falls directly onto you and me.

Writing a book about the banking industry has been a priority of mine for the last four years. Building my own business in educating and helping as many families as possible has made this adventure a long process. But it is as timely as ever. Freeing people from banks and debt has become a true passion for me.

The words of Crosby, Stills and Nash: "Teach your children well," are as timely as ever, and I encourage every reader of this book to do just that. The message herein is both clear and simple.

I have always had a passion for sharing with children what I've come to understand. I've been blessed with a great life filled with happiness and success because I was fortunate to have wonderful parents. They encouraged me to be honest and to always bring ethics and integrity to everything I do. I value these lessons far more than how much or how little money I have. Money made without ethics and integrity leads to a life of misery and unhappiness.

I've discovered that the power of association is worth discussing. It is evident that who your children's friends are will profoundly affect their futures. This is as important in adulthood. In fact, we become much like the five people we associate with the most. "Show me your friends and I'll show you your future," is certainly true and greatly impacts how we go forward positively in our financial lives.

If your closest friends believe that money is the root of all evil, you will likely never accumulate any and risk becoming a slave to it instead. Alternatively, if you spend time with successful people, you will be inspired and motivated to do as well yourself.

In the words of Warren Buffett: "It is better to hang out with people better than you. Pick out associates whose behavior is better than yours and you will drift in that direction."

In this regard, finding a mentor can be invaluable.

I've been fortunate to have met many men and women who have accumulated great fortunes without ever having sacrificed their values to do so. I've chosen these people as my mentors in business. They were very clear that the only path to enjoying their wealth was through honesty in every transaction. They never made an exception or looked the other way to make a few extra bucks. I am forever indebted to these men and women and will continue to spread their wisdom to all I meet.

I have spent more than thirteen years studying this subject, and today I can finally say that I actually understand how money works. And I have made a commitment to never stop learning.

It is my sincerest wish that what you have read here will be helpful in your finding financial freedom in your life, and the lives of your family and friends.

CPSIA information can be obtained at www.ICGtesting.com
Printed in the USA
BVOW08s1643300614

357708BV00006B/11/P

9 780578 142722